THE
Old Photographs
SERIES

BANBURY

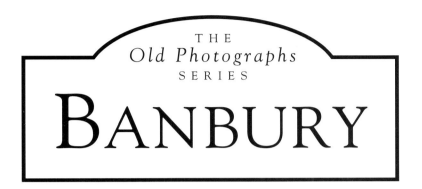

THE
Old Photographs
SERIES

BANBURY

Compiled by
Tom Rigby

**ALAN
SUTTON**

BATH • AUGUSTA • RENNES

First published 1994
Copyright © Tom Rigby1994

Alan Sutton Limited
12 Riverside Court
Bath BA2 3DZ

ISBN 0 7524 0013 4

Typesetting and origination
by Alan Sutton Limited
Printed in Great Britain

An aerial view of Banbury with the Cross and surrounding town taken in 1946.

Contents

BANBURY.

'Dominus nobis sol scutum.' (The Lord is our Sun and Shield).

Introduction

For whatever reason, be it the nursey rhyme, the food and drink, its reputation in agriculture and industry or simply because it is set in some of the most beautiful countryside in Britain, everyone knows Banbury.

This pictorial record, a trip down memory lane, contains photographs dating from the late nineteenth and early twentieth centuries when Banbury was one of the most prosperous market towns in the country, the unchallenged capital of a thriving and extensive agricultural region.

Over the years it has been celebrated for its political zeal, the innovative skills of its craftsmen, the diversity of its cultural life but perhaps most of all for the people that have made this town what it is today. Characters such as Theodore Lamb and Little Titch have added to the colourful past, right through from the early domination of the church to the devastating effect of the Civil War in 1644, from the Two World Wars to the construction of the M40.

Inevitably the town has had to move on with the times - the different cultures, the ever-changing technology, the development of transport. During the post-war era the town has benefitted from the communications explosion and been dominated by incoming industrialists but never at any time has it lost sight of its heritage and rich local history.

Banbury is geographically well-placed and has developed from a small country town into an industrial centre. The population has increased dramatically over the last one hundred and forty years from a mere 7,366 in 1841 to todays estimate of over 40,000.

Much of the town centre plan has avoided change since the Danes first invaded in AD 851. While most towns suffer a complete face-change, Banbury has expanded outwards and the facade of the original buildings often remains unchanged.

Compiling this collection of photographs, in what is my adopted home town, has been an interesting and enjoyable experience and given many hours of pleasure. It is hoped that the reader will also experience as much pleasure and be left with an indelible impression.

Tom Rigby
May 1994

Acknowledgements

During the compilation of this book I had the pleasure of working with Christine Kelly, Assistant Curator at Banbury Museum, whose knowledge of the town and its characters and relentless enthusiasm for the project were invaluable.

My thanks also go to several other people, without whose kind help and support, this book might have taken me even longer to compile. They are Nuala La Vertue at the Oxfordshire Photographic Archives, Mike Rigby, Steph Lander and June Allcock.

The majority of the photographs are reproduced by kind permission of the Oxfordshire Photographic Archive and Banbury Musem, to whom I am greatly indebted. But most of all I am indebted to the people of Banbury, to whom this book is dedicated.

One
Banbury Characters

Local farmer Francis Rathbone and two of his prize bullocks at the Fatback Christmas Show of 1926.

A crowd gathers outside the White Hart Inn on Bridge Street (McDonalds and Superdrug now stand on the site) in 1910. The landlord at the time was a Mr Jakeman, who had previously been the stationmaster at the London and North-west station.

Boxing was as common at fairs as the ferris-wheel and the merry-go-round. This menacing-looking bunch were what punters faced as they stepped into the ring at the Banbury fair of 1900.

George Herbert (1814-1902), local shoemaker and author of a book "Shoemaker's Window", a collection of memories of his early life in the town and letters written to friends around the country. This picture is taken three years before his death, soon after the completion and publication of the book.

Author, George Herbert and his musical friends pictured in about 1854. From left to right are: Charles Neighbour, violin; George Gardner, violincello; George Herbert, viola; George Partleton, violin; John Cheney, flute.

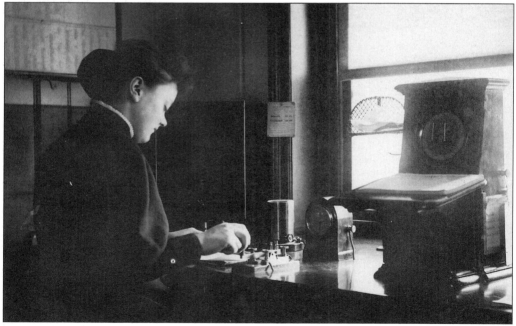

The Electric Telegraph, then owned by a private company, came to the town in 1857 and had an office in the Market Place. By the time this photograph was taken, the system was State-owned and had moved to the Post Office. This machine operator was photographed in the late 1890s.

The St Paul's Church choir in 1895. In 1851-2 Banbury saw the building of two churches, Christ Church at the junction of the present George and Broad Streets and the other, St Paul's, just outside the town's boundary at Neithrop. Elizabeth Wyatt of Linden House laid the foundation stone of St Paul's on 24 May 1852. The church was opened for services on 7 February 1853 and had average congregations of a thousand.

Local girl, Hilda Giles, pictured in costume in 1911.

Maltsters at the Hunt Edmunds Brewery in 1872. By the beginning of the nineteenth century, brewing was becoming increasingly important in the area, coming second only to the iron foundries as a source of employment. In 1823, three establishments were recorded and by 1852 this had increased to fourteen. In 1807, a brewery (later to become Hunt Edmunds) was founded by a Cropedy farmer, Thomas Hunt, who for a time ran a malting business at the Unicorn. In 1847 he moved to Bridge Street and three years later William Edmunds became a partner. From 1884, the brewery began to buy up their competitors and when in 1918 they purchased the only surviving brewery in Banbury, Messrs Drinnell & Co, they had become one of the leading brewers in Europe. In 1967, brewing in Banbury ceased when Hunt Edmunds was taken over by Mitchells & Butler. The building has since been demolished.

Eva Giles, aged 20, sister of Hilda seen on the previous page.

Employees at the Head Post Office in Banbury, 1920. The Banbury post office was successively at the Three Tuns (now Whateley Hall), White Lion and in Parson's Street before moving to its existing home in High Street in 1849. In 1935 the frontage of the building went through a total face-lift.

The Conservative Party headquarters, High Street, during the elections of January 1910. Captain R.B.Brassey was the victorious candidate.

Employees of Alcan Aluminium at a 25 Years Club party in 1958.

The new dealers' Cattle Market joins the existing cattle auction at Midland Marts, Grimsbury in 1931. Previously cattle were sold by dealers in the streets in and around Horsefair. Banbury's cattle market is now the largest in Europe. The Minister of Agriculture makes an opening speech.

St Mary's Church choir. The present St Mary's was built by Samuel Cockerill and was consecrated by Edward Smallwell, the Bishop of Oxford in 1797. It was twenty-five years before enough money was raised to build a tower. The church went through a face-lift in 1858 and by 1881 was complete as we see it today.

Employees at the Britannia Ironworks, Fish Street in 1910. It was Bernhard Samuelson who changed Banbury from a market town to an industrial centre. He had run a locomotive works in France and seen the use of labour-saving machinery. The Britannia Works occupied three sites – Upper (the site of the original shop), Canal Side and Lower (between Upper Windsor Street and the canal), connected by tramway, and by 1871 was employing 500 workers. Areas of new housing for the workers grew up in the Cherwell area and Grimsbury. Despite the depression of the late 1870s, the works continued production until 1933 and in the nineteenth century cornered much of the world market.

Banbury's traditional Michaelmas Fair attracted farmers, labourers, dealers, showmen and pickpockets from all over England. A charter of 1554 confirmed the Thursday market and granted the town the right to hold two fairs a year. As a cattle sale it declined in the 1830s and Banbury cheese was sold for the last time in 1847. It exists today as a funfair.

Every town has one! Theodore Lamb (1880-1950) was a solitary eccentric though educated character who lived in a battered old hen-house in a field off Brailes Road. Locally known as the Banbury Caveman, he wore tattered sacks, plastered his long hair with mud and rubbed lard into his skin to keep warm. He was often seen riding into town on his bicycle without rubber tyres, pulling a trolley of pots and pans behind him. He would busk in the Market Place playing the melodian and tin whistle (though not very well) but also made money from visitors to the town who came from miles around to see him. He would speak to you for one shilling and pose for a photograph for a half-crown. He also earnt money repairing watches and clocks. Men going away to war in 1914 left their watches with him for safe-keeping! Theodore was believed to have been jilted at the altar after which he went home and put on a sackcloth. Eventually the police banned him from the town because his state of dress. He died of pneumonia in 1950 at the age of seventy.

Theodore with his gramophone.

A studio photograph of a local midget known
as Little Titch taken in about 1906.

The Banbury Co-operative Society Management Committee pictured with Alderman W.Mascord, town Mayor in 1929.

Reverend R.M.Pope of the Marlborough Road Methodist Church.

Members of the Banbury Bowling Club in 1890.

Mr J.Perry pictured in 1920 in his official
capacity as Mayor of Banbury.

A group of lady members from the Co-operative Society representing various countries in a World Peace pageant in the early 1920s.

The Co-operative Society Choir on the roof of Central Stores at the corner of Broad Street and George Street in about 1920.

John Hobbs, the town's bell-ringer, pictured in 1850 with his handbells mounted on a half-barrel.

A Sunday afternoon gathering outside the Barley Mow public house on the Drayton Road in 1912. The sign announcing that teas were served at moderate prices shows how formal and polite was advertising at the beginning of the century.

Two
Ride a Cock Horse...

Looking West up the High Street in 1905. Before the advent of railways, coaches were the means of long-distance travel and seven turnpike roads passed through Banbury. The Red Lion (seen on the left of the picture) was one of the most notable inns and at one time it operated as the post office. It survived the fire of 1628 and the Civil War to be demolished in 1930 to make way for a new Woolworth store, but this too is now gone. The shops shown on the South side of the High Street were once the South side of the Market Place.

Town Hall and the Cattle Market, 1878. The foundation stone for the new town hall (the fourth to be built) in Bridge Street was laid by Mayor Thomas Draper on 29th July 1853. The siting was originally controversial because it was built on the site of an old refuse pit. It cost £3,386 to build. In 1860 a clock was added and in 1889 the hall was extended to accommodate a new council chamber. For some years the building housed the police station and the magistrates court before their move to the present site in the Warwick Road. The previous town hall, which had stood in the centre of the Market Place since about 1800, was removed to Lower Cherwell Street where it is still used as a warehouse.

South Bar, Banbury

Construction work on St John's Church on South Bar began in 1835 and the first Mass said by Bishop Wiseman on 19th June 1837. Local Protestants and Nonconformists took every opportunity to express the displeasure at Roman Catholicism and burned an effigy of Dr Tandy, the priest responsible for the completion of the building. When a pinnacle fell during high winds it was taken to be a sign. They were subsequently reduced in size but have since been taken down altogether.

The site of the thatched cottages on the left of the photograph was taken over by the Co-operative Society in 1908. Towering above the cottages in 1900 was Christ Church, opened as the parish church of South Banbury in 1853, after the ecclesiastical parish was divided. It was demolished in 1970.

The interior of the Wesleyan Chapel, built in 1864, in Marlborough Road following increased demand of Wesleyans in the town. It was by far the largest Nonconformist place of worship in Banbury.

Cattle being driven towards the market. A familiar sight in the late 1890s.

A view from around 1900 looking from the west end of Parson's Street, so-called because many of its buildings were owned by the Church. It has been home to slaughterhouses (removed in 1865) and to the Cuttle Brook, which flowed down the street, forming a pool in the Market Place, where scolds, fraudulent bakers and pickpockets were ducked until 1830 when a woman died in the stool.

The shape of Parson's Street has remained the same for centuries. This picture, taken in 1923, shows two famous landmarks – on the left, Ye Olde Reindeer Inn the oldest building in Banbury and opposite, the original cake shop.

The Town Hall looking up from Bridge Street in the early 1920s.

Opposite: This picture taken in 1958 looks through to High Street from the Market Place, and shows the Greek-style pillars of the Baptist Chapel. It is said that before it was a chapel it was a tavern and, although unlikely, legend has it that William the Conqueror stayed here. Today the former Chapel is a shop and the buildings on the left of the picture have been redeveloped and house the National Westminster Bank.

A sad day for Banbury. After two hundred years of baking, the original cake shop is reduced to a pile of rubble. In 1968, while under the ownership of the long-standing Brown family (resident since 1872), the cake shop was sold to developers and before a preservation order could be confirmed the building was destroyed.

Nothing much has changed since this sweeping view of South Bar was taken in 1912 although the grass verge is now taken up by car parking spaces.

Until the early 1930s cattle were sold in Broad Street but that was long before this picture was taken in 1964.

The Original Banbury Cake Shop pictured in 1955. The town has long been renowned for its cakes, possibly back to before the reign of Elizabeth I. During the mid-nineteenth century the shop was owned by Samuel Beesley who exported his cakes to America, Australia and India.

Central Stores with its impressive clock tower built for the Co-operative Society on the corner of Broad Street and George Street. Built in 1908 it is today the home to Rylands. The corner entrance, seen here in about 1916, no longer exists.

Parson's Street showing the original cake shop, Ye Olde Reindeer Inn and the former offices of the Banbury Guardian in about 1930.

High Street through to Bridge Street in 1890. This street is now pedestrianised.

Banbury GWR Station in 1905. Banbury's importance as a regional centre was a direct result of the coming of the railways. The Buckinghamshire Railway opened on 1st May 1850, beating the GWR by a few months. The GWR opened to Banbury on 2nd September with a service to Paddington of a little over two and a half hours.

Merton Street Station in about 1953. On the London North Western Railway line it was one of two stations in the town and was closed in December 1964.

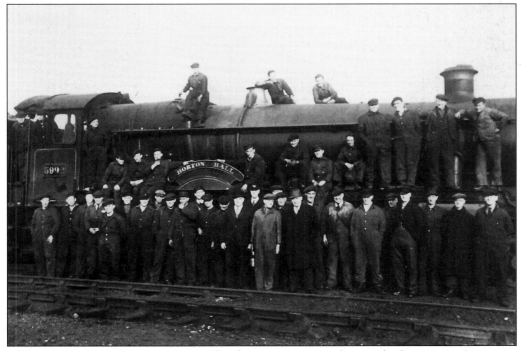

This picture of GWR engineering staff with an engine was taken in the late 1940s. Sitting on the footplate are T.Wyatt and G.Maycock.

Looking South along the platform of the Great Western Railway Station in 1905.

The Oxford Road has not changed much since this photograph was taken in 1921. The houses lining the right hand side of the street are now predominantly guest houses.

Middleton Road, seen here in about 1920, is a continuation of Bridge Street, beyond the railway bridge, in the suburb of Grimsbury.

The White Lion Hotel on High Street, pictured here in 1887, was a prominent coaching inn. The wide gateway and courtyard (now White Lion Walk) was used by London-bound coaches for a change of horses. It also housed the Post Office during the eighteenth century. The white lion above the gateway still stands although the hotel has closed.

North Bar pictured in the early 1930s. There are few changes to be seen but Stranks Restaurant and the Commercial Hotel are now better known as the Buck and Bell public house. In the early part of the century Stranks owned a simple boarding house next door providing a popular breakfast stop for delivery men and early risers. The newsagents on the corner of Parson's Street still exists.

Opposite: West Bar Street was originally known as Shokersford or Shookewell and in later years as Sugarford Bar and Bull Bar, after a local inn. The Gothic terraces and villas on West Bar were much sought after by the wealthy during the 1860s and 70s.

This picture of Bridge Street taken in 1924 looks towards the railway station from the foot of the Town Hall. To the far left of the photograph you can just make out what is now the bus station.

Upper Windsor Street in the mid-1920s.

Three
To See a Fine Lady...

Banbury Cross pictured in 1900. The present cross was built in Horsefair in 1859 and does not lie on the site of any of the three earlier crosses - the High or Market Cross, the Bread Cross or the White Cross. It was built to commemorate the marriage of the Princess Royal, Victoria Adelaide Maria Louise, to Albert Frederick William, Prince of Prussia on 25th January 1858. There was great controversy as to whether a cross or fountain should be built and eventually a compromise was reached when J. Gibbs of Oxford was commissioned to design the present neo-Gothic cross. Here the railings can be seen, added in 1888, but the statues of King George V, Edward VII and Queen Victoria were to appear later to mark King George's coronation in 1911.

Ride a Cock Horse
To Banbury Cross
To see a Fine Lady
On a White Horse
Rings on her Fingers
Bells on her Toes
She shall have Music
Wherever She goes

Disappointing as it may be for visitors, the cross that we see today is not the original one nor the one mentioned in the nursery rhyme but, in fact, the fourth Banbury Cross to be built in the town. The cross of the rhyme is said to have stood near the Corn Exchange in the Market Place and was pulled down by the Puritans in 1602. One version of the legend says that the rhyme refers to the ride from London made by Celia Fiennes in 1698, an ancestor of intrepid explorer Sir Ranulph. The Fiennes family still lives at nearby Broughton Castle. An alternative and popular theory is that the fine lady with rings and bells was Lady Godiva, the famous wife of the Earl of Mercia.

Looking North towards the Cross in around 1878. Over the years Banbury Cross has created increasing traffic problems for the town even resulting in threats to remove it! The gas lamps in this picture were installed in November 1859 to protect unwary travellers from bumping into the cross on foggy nights.

Diamond Jubilee celebrations at the Cross in 1897.

A little girl stands against the lamp-post at the Cross with St Mary's in the background. A very different scene to that of the busy Cross junction today, *c.*1895.

Four

Those Who Served

The Northern Aluminium Company Rescue team of 1940.

The Banbury Police Force of 1927.

Children stare wide-eyed and follow the drummer as the Royal Hussars parade through town.

The Oxon Royal Hussars parade down High Street in 1905.

The Banbury Home Guard pictured at Whateley Hall during the Second World War. Banbury was a target for enemy bombs because of the aluminium factory which was supplying materials for allied aircraft. The Civil Defence and Home Guard organisations built a dummy factory at Hardwick which was hit by bombs in August of 1940. In October of the same year, six people were killed when a bomb from a Dornier bomber hit a signal box at the railway station.

A group of ex-servicemen pictured in 1918. The First World War had a dramatic effect on the town. In all, 2,161 Banburians served in the forces and 326 of them never returned.

Members of the local detachment of the Red Cross are pictured at Alcan during World War Two.

A scene in a ward at Horton General Hospital during the Christmas of 1908. The hospital was opened in 1872 with funds provided by Miss Horton of the Holt, Middleton Cheney. She died before the hospital was finished but her family saw to it that her wishes were carried out.

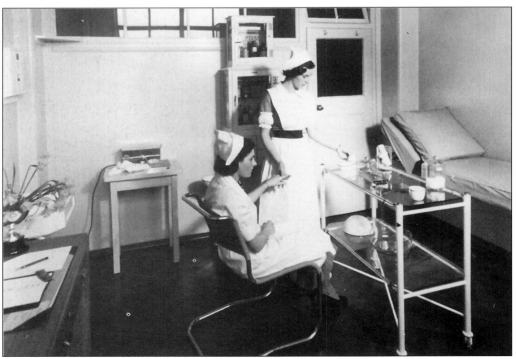

The surgery at Spencer's Corsets factory on Britannia Road in 1930.

High Constable Tustain pictured in uniform in 1880.

The Borough Police Force pictured in 1925. Following the 1835 local election Parliament passed the Municipal Corporations Act and by the following year an efficient police force had been formed by the Town Council consisting of six watchmen, four petty constables, two constables and a superintendent. Before this revolution crime had been rife within the town.

The Banbury Volunteer Fire Brigade (BVFG) pictured at the rear of Whateley Hall in 1880. In 1859 a large part of the south side of the Cow Fair between the brewery and the Crown was burnt out and engines had to be called from neighbouring towns to augment the parish engines.

Here they show off their latest fire engine in about 1910.

An official BVFB photograph from the early part of this century.

The BVFB outside the Hunt Edmunds Malthouse in the early 1890s.

Firemen and appliances ready for inspection outside their headquarters in 1955.

The first regular BVFB outside the Town Hall in 1870. Until 1852 fire-fighting had been a parish concern.

The Banbury division of the British Legion parade in People's Park in about 1935.

Doctors and volunteer nurses at the Red Cross Hospital on West Street in about 1915.

Five
The Market Place

Banbury Market Place in the 1920s.

The market on a beautiful day in 1918. Although much of the centre of town was altered or rebuilt between 1850 and 1880 as it grew into a major market town, most of the principal retailers and inns remained grouped here for centuries. To this day it remains the focal point of the town and on market days (Thursday and Saturday) resembles a hive of bees. It has also played host to the greatest fair in the South Midlands.

Fairs have always played an important part in the town. The annual Michaelmas Fair is held in the Market Place and this picture from 1902 shows how the centre of town was brought to a standstill by the stalls and rides.

Market Place looking from the East in 1910.

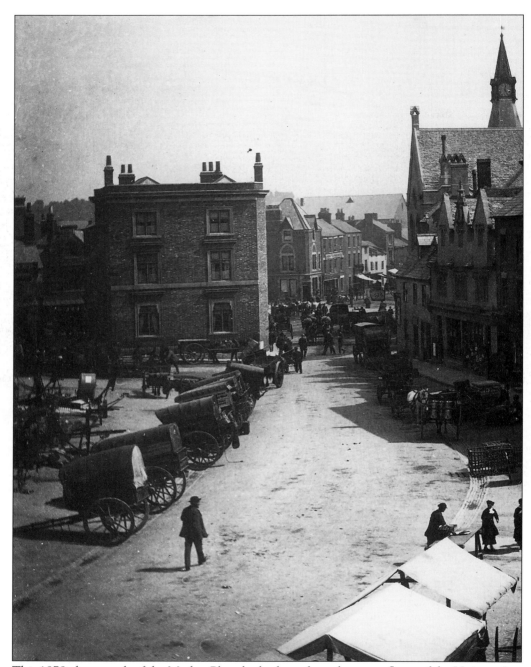

This 1878 photograph of the Market Place looks down from the upper floors of the Unicorn Inn and allows a good view of the roadway leading through to Bridge Street. It is amazing just how little has changed. The building with three gables (right of centre) housed the former Banbury gaol. After it's conditions were described as among the worst in the country, it was closed in 1852 and the prisoners removed to Oxford. In 1854 its residual function as an overnight lock-up was replaced by cells in the new town hall. The Blue Coat School was above the gaol until 1817 after which the pupils attended the National School in Southam Road.

This view from the South side of the Market Place in about 1922 shows the area known as Cornhill. A large part of the town's history is represented in this small area. Just left of centre are William Wilkinson's Gothic houses built in 1866 and in the centre is the building formerly occupied by Gilletts Bank. The adjoining stone building to the right was formerly the Plough Inn, while on the extreme right of the square is the facade of the Cornhill Corn Exchange, built in 1857 to rival the Central Corn Exchange just across the way. Neither exchanges were successful and through the years the Cornhill building played host to a number of businesses including an auction and the Vine Inn. Cornhill is where the famous High Cross stood (of which the rhyme speaks) and where the first town hall stood for many years. This is also the site of the celebrated Cheese Fair referred to by Shakespeare. The ornate front of the Corn Exchange now forms the entrance to the Castle Shopping Centre and the statue that stands at its peak is of Ceres, the goddess of corn. The original statue had its head blown off in a gale at the turn of the century and was only replaced in 1981.

A busy Thursday market in 1953.

Looking East down through Market Place in about 1910. The shops on the left are Sheasby & Sons, Broughton & Wilks the ironmongers, and Durran's earthenware shop. The building that stands alone at the far end of the Market Place was Gillett's Bank and also home to its chief clerk Mr Barrett.

Looking along the West side of the Market Place in 1926. From left to right: the shop on the corner, here owned by the Robins Bros. Ironmongers, is one of the towns oldest surviving buildings, next is a corsetry shop, undoubtedly supplied by the local Spencer's Corsets. The adjoining archway was once the entrance to the Central Corn Exchange and has the old 'Sun in Glory' town emblem carved in its stone. Later it was to become the entrance to Blinkholm's Picture House until it was replaced by the Palace Arcade and with the advent of cinema, the Palace Cinema in 1916. Halfords, the cycle specialists, have now moved to High Street. Next is the three-bay windowed building of the Unicorn Inn, one of the earliest and most important buildings to be erected after the Civil war. It once occupied the whole of the gabled building, before shops such as Kays moved in, and then were replaced by the Midland Bank and the Nationwide Building Society. The inn is still selling beer and can be found through the beautifully carved gateway, dated 1648.

By the time this photograph was taken in the 1930s, Kays Modern Food Stores had moved into the front of the old Unicorn Inn and were announcing their arrival with gusto! The cinema was still in the building on the left although many of the shops have by now changed hands.

A corner of the Market Place in about 1878. Wares are displayed for sale on the ground and from stalls. A crowd is gathering around one stall in the foreground, perhaps to hear an auctioneer or to listen to a particularly entertaining trader.

015 Tradition has it that the shop on the corner of Market Place and Parson's Street (just left of centre) is the prebendal or rectory house (much restored) built in 1665. For many years it was a drapers, clothiers and furnishers owned by a succession of companies such as Powell's and Harlock's. Today it is a British Gas showroom. This photograph was taken in about 1920.

Cornhill in 1902.

Six
Market Town Trade

Staff of T.W.Coleman's family grocers stand outside the shop in 1900.

Sheep market at a Horse Fair in about 1900.

Alfred Betts' Cake shop on High Street pictured in 1900. The coat of arms above the shop name signifies that he was appointed as purveyor to Her Majesty Queen Victoria. The shop now houses Lunn Poly the travel agents.

The Original Cake Shop on Parson's Street is decorated for the Coronation of Edward VII in 1902.

A look inside the men's bakehouse at Browns in 1959. Mrs Brown was a strict Quaker and segregated her workers. Only men were allowed to make Banbury cakes while the ladies were left to concentrate on the icing and pastries. George Bennett is on the left and Wilfred Brow is holding the tray of cakes.

Nunbers 2-4 Market Place, seen here in about 1906, were formerly the town gaol and the Fox Inn.

Members of the Banbury Co-operative Industrial Society stand outside the shop at its opening ceremony in 1900.

Banbury Co-operative Industrial Society in around 1920.

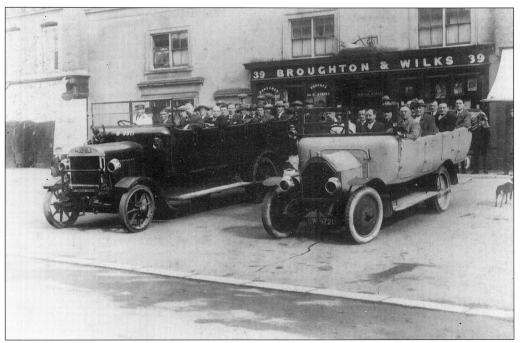

Banbury Butchers Association setting off on an outing in charabancs in 1924.

Staff at Kilby's Cooperage on Southam Road in 1913.

Robin Brothers, ironmongers and hardware dealers, in the Market Place in about 1912.

The Leathern Bottle public house stood on the site of the present Bus Station in Castle Street and was demolished in the early 1950s.

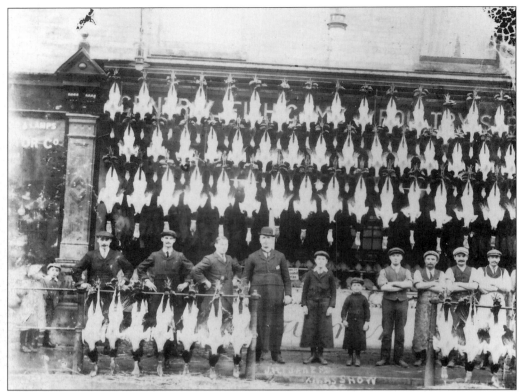

J.H. Turner's shop on Broad Street had been supplying the community with fish, game and poultry for many years when this photograph of his Christmas Show was taken in 1905.

Staff at Kilby's Cooperage in 1925.

The courtyard at the rear of the Reindeer Inn during the early part of this century. The Globe Room, which was added in 1637, is on the right. It is thought that the famous Civil War picture captioned, 'When did you last see your Father?', had the Globe Room as its background. In the early twentieth century the fine ornamental panelling was removed and exported to America. It was traced by the Banbury Historical Society and bought back by the Banbury Borough Council and is now in the Museum. This photograph is from about 1890.

Carriers such as Harry Bonham, seen here in about 1910, continued to play a vital role in the town trade well into the twentieth century. They would bring goods for sale from the villages and take back goods required by villagers thus forming an important link between town and country. As the railways and other types of transport began to improve their work began to diminish.

Ye Olde Reindeer Inn dates back to the mid-sixteenth century when it was a stone building with a timber-framed front to the upper storey. The front block and three-storey wing were added in 1570 with ovolo sectioned windows. The inscription above the magnificent gates reads 'IOHN-KNIGHT + IHONE-KNIGHT + DAVID-HORN. ANNO DIN 1570'.

Nathan's Domestic Store on the South side of Market Place pictured in the mid-1950s.

Market Place looking towards Cornhill in about 1878.

W.H.Hobbs, dealer in oils and hardware, with his delivery van in 1920.

The staff outside W.H.Smith & Son, 94 High Street, in 1915. As well as a stationers and newsagents the shop was also a library.

The Banbury rock-maker, J.H.Leach, stands in the doorway of his shop on High Street.

The Banbury Co-operative Society based at Bloxham in about 1905.

Employees at Britannia Works in 1910.

Numbers 86-87 High Street in about 1884.

Opposite: Alcan Aluminium factory on Hardwick Hill in 1949. The lack of employment opportunities became acute during the late 1920s and so when the Borough Treasurer heard that the Northern Aluminium Company was looking for a site for a rolling mill, negotiations went ahead. The new mill came into operation in November 1931 and through the Second World War played an important part in providing aluminium for Spitfires and Bailey bridges. Work continued seven days a week with a break on Saturdays to allow the furnaces to be cleaned. With the arrival of Alcan much new house buildingtook place at Ruscote, to provide for the influx of labour. By the begining of the War the population of Banbury had risen to 18,000, an increase of 4,000 in eight years. In 1938 Aluminium Laboratories Ltd built new premises for research which were greatly extended in 1952.

Employees at Hunt Edmunds Brewery in 1950.

The factory floor at Spencer's Corsets in 1930.

Brown's butchers shop and staff in 1920.

Staff at J. H. Thornton, wholesale and retailers, stand outside the shop in 1930.

Croughton's Butcher's with Mr Cave standing at the market stall in about 1910.

Eyre's yeast shop in the Market Place opened in 1896 and closed in 1964.

Simcoe & Tite were high-class bootsellers at 68 Bridge Street during the 1900s.

Numbers 85-87 High Street in the mid-1860s. The corner shop was later to become Alfred Betts' Cake Shop. At the time of this photograph his father William was trading at his famous cake shop at 70 High Street.

A horse and delivery cart belonging to J.Hobbs, dealer in paint and varnish, stands outside the shop in Monument Street at the turn of the century.

Drapery was an important and fashionable industry during the early part of this century. Francis' and Harlock's (now the gas showroom) were just two of several in the area surrounding the Market Place in this picture from about 1910.

High Street butchers, Giles & Son and their very smart delivery carts. *c.* 1918.

Seven
Schooldays

A woodwork class at the County School on Marlborough Road, now the library, in 1925.

A girls art lesson in the top room of the County School in 1922.

The British School designed by J.M.Derrick was housed on Crouch Street on the western side of South Bar. It was one of the first buildings to be constructed in this new housing area in 1839. This painting was completed in 1890.

St John's School was opened as a day school in 1846 by Dr Tandy and was conducted by Sisters whom he had secured from the Community of St Paul at Chartres. In 1849 the adjacent building was purchased and the Priory School started. This picture of a class was taken in 1905.

A commemorative tree is planted in the grounds of the newly-named County School on Marlborough Road, after the Municipal School was handed over to the County Council as a maintained school. In 1930, the school was moved to new premises in Easington and the school of Art and Evening Classes remained at Marlborough Road. The buildings were later redeveloped as the Banbury Technical College.

Children from Cherwell Infants School taking part in a concert at the turn of the century.

Some of the teaching staff at the County School during the mid-1920s.

The teaching staff at Banbury School in the early 1920s. The story begins in 1893 when due largely to the inspiration of Bernhard Samuelson, owner of the Britannia Works and the local MP, a secondary and technical school was opened in an extension of the existing School of Science and Art. Today's library is housed in these original buildings. Together they formed the Municipal School, later to become Banbury School. It was opened on July 4th 1893 by the Right Hon. Herbert C. Gardener MP, who was then President of the Board of Agriculture. At the ceremony it was announced that Samuelson was to be knighted for his services in the promotion of technical education in the country.

Pupils at the Municipal School pose for the year photograph in June of 1920. Note that these photographs are two halves of one picture.

These seven little girls were pupils at Britannia Road Infants School in 1920. The picture was taken during a concert sketch entitled 'Bluebells'. They are, from left to right: Vera Charles, Flo Blackwell, Kate Stone, Frances Mobbs, May Kirkland, Kath Puffet and Gertie Neville.

A woodwork class at the County School in 1922.

Studio portrait of Mrs J.A.Bowkett Headmistress of Cherwell Infants School in 1905.

Mrs Bowkett and the 'Baby Class' at Cherwell Infants School in 1905.

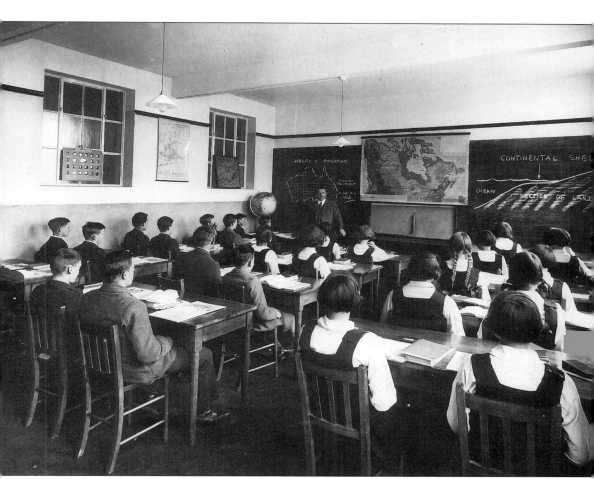

A top year geography class at the County School in 1934.

These young boys and girls from Class Three are pictured outside Grimsbury Council Infants' School in 1915.

The First Grimsbury Scout Group founded in 1948.

A group of brickyard workers and their families in the early 1920s. The men from left to right are: Paddy, W.Plester, G.Kite, W.Dale, T.Holton, G.Boswell (foreman) and L.Ward. The children are: R.Boswell, B.Cork, P.Cork, J.Thompson and Miss Kite.

A group of pupils in costume outside the Britannia Road School at Christmas 1910.

A recorder lesson at St Leonards School in 1962.

A prizegiving ceremony attended by the Mayor at the County School in the early 1920s.

Dashwood Road School.

Pupils in the playground at Dashwood Road School in around 1905.

Children perform in theatrical costume at Cherwell Infants School in the early part of this century.

Eight
Sports and Celebrations

The ferris-wheel and merry-go-round at the Michaelmas Fair in 1905.

Looking West up High Street during preparations for the celebrations commemorating Victoria's Diamond Jubilee in 1897.

The Neithrop Wesleyan Sunday School parades up to the Market Place from Bridge Street in 1897.

Four ladies wearing clothing advertising Co-op products in readiness for the Michaelmas Fair during the 1920s.

Parson's Street is decorated in grand style for Queen Victoria's Diamond Jubilee in 1897.

R.Wilson & Sons merry-go-round at the Michaelmas fair in 1952.

This float was part of a church parade in 1900.

The annual Northern Aluminium Company sports day in about 1950.

The Municipal School cricket team in 1922.

Banbury Spencer Football Club womens' team show their colours during the 1950s.

Great Western Railway Reserves football team in the 1922/23 season.

A happier side to life during the 1940s. These Banbury football supporters made a day of it when they went to see Banbury Spencer take on the might of Oxford City in the F.A. Cup. Banbury went on to win the match 5-0.

Banbury Football Club (and mascot), 1896-87.

These Romany-like folks led by Mrs Rebecca Watson (centre, wearing a brimmed hat), owner of Watson's Off Licence, were gathered in High Street during one of the many fund-raising efforts for Horton General Hospital during the mid-1930s.

North Street celebrates VJ Day with a street party in 1945.

Children in costume parade around the town in a their quest to raise money for the hospital in these two pictures from the 1930s.

The annual Banbury Pageant parades through High Street on a day in the 1920s.

A crowd gathers outside the Liberal Party headquarters during the last election of the century in 1900. Mr Albert Brassey the Conservative candidate eventually beat the Liberal candidate, the Hon Eustace Fiennes, by 3,632 to 2,821 votes.

St Leonards football team during the 1924/25 season.

High Street prepares for the parties during the Diamond Jubilee celebrations of 1897.

The Banbury Co-op Womens Guild formal dinner, in a room festooned with flags and bunting. What was the celebration? Lord Mayor W.Mascord is seated to the left of centre. The date is around 1929.

This float was a favourite at the Diamond Jubilee celebrations in 1897. As it travelled around the town it handed out cakes to the crowds that had gathered along the streets.

A church procession through the town during the early part of the century.